12/2005

MW01258355

Merry
Christmas!
Marla!

Gayle

TIFFANY FLORA

TIFFANY FLORA

John Loring

HARRY N. ABRAMS, INC., PUBLISHERS

Columbine and passion-
flower studies from a Tiffany
School album in the Tiffany
archives, c. 1890.

"UMBRELLA" MAGNOLIA

SHOWING BUD, TOP & SIDE VIEWS

CONTENTS

"MOTHER NATURE IS THE BEST DESIGNER."

This adage has been the unofficial motto of Tiffany design throughout its history, just as "Good design is good business" has been its succinctly put merchandising philosophy, first articulated by Charles Lewis Tiffany, who founded the company in New York in 1837. Throughout history, Mother Nature has both endowed the North American continent with unparalleled riches and has served as a primary inspiration in the establishment of a national style of art and design.

Tiffany's prominent role in American design emerged around 1870, some five years after the conclusion of the Civil War, when the company's head designer, Edward C. Moore, established one of the United States's first schools of design at Tiffany's new flagship store, which had just opened on the southwest corner of New York's Fifteenth Street and Union Square. Moore, who later achieved international recognition at the Paris Exposition of 1878 for his Japanesque silverwares, put together a design collection for his Tiffany School of applied art that was at the time the greatest of its kind in America. It included thousands of Near Eastern and Oriental art objects as well as books on drawing and ornament, an important collection of early botanical photographs, and studies on the adaptation of plant and animal forms to the applied arts. Botanical specimens were regularly brought to the Tiffany School and meticulous pencil and watercolor studies were drawn by the student-apprentices and added to the school's design collection. Preserved in the Tiffany Archives, they constitute a uniquely rich collection of nineteenth-century American botanical drawing.

Moore was a man of his times and kept his Tiffany School abreast of developments in the world of art and design on both sides of the Atlantic. He frequently traveled to Paris and

Orchid Brooch Number 66
designed by Paulding Farnham and
made in 1890, based on a study that
he labeled *Cleisostoma ionusmum.*

London to add to both his personal and teaching collections and, while abroad in the late 1860s, he became keenly aware of the immense influence of Japanese art on the newly founded school of French Impressionism as well as on the decorative arts in general. He collected Japanese design manuals with their stylish patterns of flora and fauna abstracted from nature by Andō Hiroshige (1797–1858), Katsushika Hokusai (1760–1849), and others for use by Tiffany's designers.

Curiously, however, Moore's collection for Tiffany's design students did not seem to have included the illustrated publications of the early American naturalists such as Alexander Wilson (1766–1813), Thomas Say (1787–1834), Titian Ramsey Peale (1799–1885), Thomas Doughty (1793–1856), or John James Audubon (1785–1851). This was possibly because their works were both already well known and readily available elsewhere in New York, or perhaps because the realistic, almost scientific precision of their art was out of step with Moore's more advanced taste for Orientalism.

Moore had visited Paris in 1867 to attend that year's Exposition, where his Tiffany silver designs won a bronze medal, the first such prize ever awarded to an American firm by an international jury. By 1867, his silver designs with stylized Persian floral motifs already showed influences of the Middle Eastern art that he had begun to collect some years earlier, and in Paris in 1867 his interest in Orientalism expanded to include Japanese art, whose influence was emerging in the Impressionist paintings of Édouard Manet (1832–1883) as well as in the celebrated ceramics of Félix Bracquemond (1833–1914), who won a gold medal at the exposition for a faïence dinner service designed for noted fellow French fancier of Japonisme and designer of glass and ceramics Eugène Rousseau (1827–1890). (The service, manufactured in 1866 for Rousseau by L. M. Creil & Cie. of Montereau, was considered the first work of Japonisme in France and included flowers taken directly from a design manual of Hokusai's *Manga* series.)

From Nature
Japanese Quince
May 1882.

Apple blossoms and Japanese quince drawn from nature at the Tiffany School, both dated May 1882. The school comprised apprentice designers at the silver factory on Prince Street in lower Manhattan working under Edward C. Moore. Its most distinguished graduates were Paulding Farnham and John T. Curran. These studies mark a departure from Edward C. Moore's flowering branches on 1870s Tiffany silverware inspired by Japanese woodblock prints, showing the transition to the more naturalistic designs of John T. Curran and Paulding Farnham in the 1880s and 1890s.

ch. aubry

Charles Aubry's photographs of Oriental poppies (opposite page), and Oriental poppies with a rose, two variegated carnations, and a budding lilac, at left. They are from an album that Aubry presented to Eugène, the Prince Imperial (son of Emperor Napoleon III of France), in 1864 to promote nature as a source for design. The album found its way to Tiffany & Co.'s design library, perhaps when the company purchased a large portion of the crown jewels auctioned by the French Ministry of Finance in May 1887.

The artists of the nineteenth-century French avant-garde found liberation from the restrictive and oppressive conventions of Second Empire academic art in the stylishly refined and simplified interpretations of nature, dramatically cropped asymmetrical compositions, flattened picture planes, and pure luminous colors of Japanese woodblock prints. Equally inspired by the austerity of the Japanese aesthetic, Moore must also have seen a brighter future for American art and design beyond the spectacular if often pompous and academic works of the romantic Hudson River School of landscape artist-explorers that dominated the New York art world from the 1850s to the 1870s.

This semiofficial school of art was, of course, a direct outgrowth of the Philadelphia school of artist-explorers that revolved around the Philadelphia Academy of Sciences. Their illustrations, beginning with Alexander Wilson's first bird prints for his *American Ornithology* in 1808 and ending with the completion of Thomas Doughty's *Cabinet of Natural History and American Rural Sports* in 1834, had laid the groundwork for the Hudson River School's Thomas Cole, Frederick Church, George Catlin, Albert Bierstadt, Thomas Moran, and Martin Johnson Heade, who made up New York's artistic pantheon at the time of Edward C. Moore's visit to Paris in 1867.

The most acclaimed of the artist-explorers, John James Audubon, lived at his estate overlooking the Hudson River near Riverside Drive and 158th Street from the time Moore was fifteen until he was twenty-four; he died in 1851, the year Moore joined Tiffany & Co. Moore was surely aware of the great naturalist's work, *The Birds of America* (published 1826–38) and of the works of the whole school of Philadelphia naturalist artist-explorers that had preceded Audubon. All were the forebears of the artists of the Hudson River School, whose allegiance, by nature of their profession, was devoted more to the interests of the federal government's projects of westward expansion and their own financial ambitions (and later to the interest of the railroads serving travel to the natural wonders of America) than to the progress of art and design. By 1867, however, the Civil War had brought an end to both the vision of the United States as an unspoiled paradise waiting to be civilized and to much of the popularity of the Hudson River School and academic (as well as romantic) naturalism.

Pioneers in their efforts to infuse Western art with Japanese aesthetics included Édouard Manet and Félix Bracquemond in Paris, the expatriate American Impressionist James Abbott McNeill Whistler in London, and Edward C. Moore in New York. In absorbing the lessons of Japan's woodblock printmakers, Moore and his collaborators in both the Tiffany School and in the Tiffany silver design department were well ahead of their time with their glorious Japanesque silverwares decorated with the elegant, graphically simplified flora and fauna of the Japanese masters reinterpreted in variously colored metals on luminous, matte, hammered-silver surfaces.

Tiffany's first Japanesque wares, which appeared around 1870, were already clearly the result of experiments during the three years since the 1867 Paris Exposition. Moore's Japanese flat silver design (now called Audubon) of Oriental birds and flowers was patented on April 18, 1871. His Japanesque wares were shown at the Philadelphia Centennial Exposition of 1876 and again two years later at the Paris Exposition, where Moore was acclaimed the uncontested world leader of silver design. Moore's Japanesque wares showed both his complete mastery of Japonisme in design and an astonishing mastery of Japanese metalworking techniques, and they were perfectly in line with the work of painters such as Manet.

Moore's advance on the aesthetic of the times is visible in a number of examples. For instance, although Hiroshige's plum blossoms had ornamented Moore's Tiffany silver as early as 1878, Vincent Van Gogh did not begin his *japonaiserie* of a plum tree in bloom after Hiroshige until 1886. Furthermore, Japanese irises were everywhere on Moore's Tiffany silver long before the painted versions of Van Gogh and Monet appeared, and Hokusai's *Hawk* (1834) was present

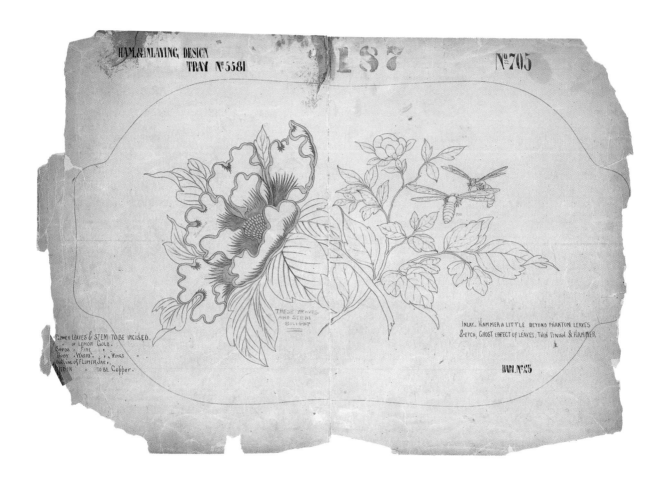

Hammering and inlaying design for peonies and bees
on a Japanesque-style silver tray designed by Edward
C. Moore, c.1878. Moore was Tiffany's chief designer
from the late 1850s until his death in 1891. Although
he probably used an actual peony as a model, he was
strongly influenced by a Hiroshige woodblock print
(opposite), from a design manual in his collection.
Peonies are traditional Buddhist symbols for the beginning of spring.

on Tiffany silver in 1878, more than ten years before Moore's friend Siegfried Bing, the leading Paris art dealer-promoter of Japonisme, published it in his *Le Japon Artistique* in August 1889.

Another remarkable floral style that Moore and his school developed for the Paris Exposition of 1878 was a richly detailed mixture of Persian, Japanese, Chinese, British, and American floral patterns exhibited on a massive 1,250-piece silver service made for Silver Bonanza King John W. MacKay. Moore called the style Saracenic, although it was an outgrowth of his less eclectic Persian-style silver shown as early as 1867 and a further development of his Persian flat silver pattern of 1872 featured in Tiffany's silver display at the Philadelphia 1876 Centennial.

Although the term *Saracenic* was already in use to describe desert nomads and their culture, Edward C. Moore may possibly have derived it as his new name for this international mixture of Orientalist patterns from the term *Sarasatic*, applied to contemporary Japanese patterns in the textile maker's reference books, or from *shōe* collections, where traditional Japanese designs began to show influences from the outside world as the international industrial revolution was sowing the seeds of world monoculture. No *shōe* books of Sarasatic patterns exist in the Tiffany archives, but five books of Japanese "wallpaper" motifs (which may well have been textile rather than wallpaper designs) were listed in Moore's inventory. In any case, Moore's daisy patterns, maple leaves, and other borders of repeated floral images on Japanesque silver suggest that the Tiffany School had Sarasatic textile-pattern books at their disposal, even if those books, like all but one of the fifteen volumes of Hokusai's *Manga*, as well as Moore's copies of Hiroshige's design manuals from which his Japanesque designs of the 1870s are derived, are missing today. In any case, Moore's Saracenic patterns were a highly eclectic mixture of Orientalist styles with occasional American and British floral motifs tossed in for good measure, loosely interpreting the arts of Islam.

Moore's Japanesque silver designs won a gold medal at the 1878 Exposition, and the market demand for these Tiffany wares remained at a high level throughout the 1880s. However, as the next great exposition, to be held in Paris in 1889, approached, the flora and fauna of Tiffany evolved away from the directions first suggested by the Tiffany School's study of Japanese printmakers and their design manuals toward a far more mimetic interpretation of nature. In the Tiffany School, this was largely due to the maturing designs of Moore's two prize students, Paulding Farnham and John T. Curran, whose years of painting botanical studies under Moore's direction began to bear fruit around 1885.

By 1885, the New York press had noted the enameled floral jewels of Tiffany's young design prodigy, "Paul" Farnham, on display at Tiffany's Union Square store. The series began, not surprisingly, with a Japanese chrysanthemum brooch but quickly moved away from Japonisme to lilacs, roses, heliotrope, mignonette, gentians, trumpet vine, and, most significantly, to orchids.

At the time, orchids were still rare, highly prized status symbols of the 1880s, at least two of Tiffany's most important customers, Jay Gould and Mary Jane Morgan, were avid collectors of orchids, and one of the Hudson River School painters, Martin Johnson Heade (1819–1904), had been making a successful career of painting orchids (usually combined with hummingbirds) since around 1870. Among the botanical studies of Edward C. Moore's Tiffany School, the drawings of orchids from the 1880s far outnumber those of any other flower group, magnolia studies being the runner-up.

Archival photograph and drawing of a gourd-shaped Japanesque silver tray with an applied iris designed by Edward C. Moore for the Paris Exposition of 1878. Gourds, gourd shapes, and irises were favorites of Moore in his Japanesque silver designs.

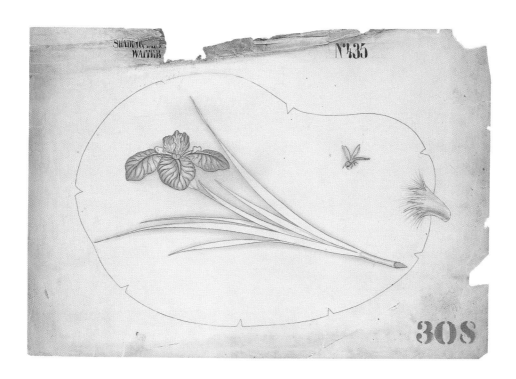

Just as Edward C. Moore had pioneered Japonisme along with the avant-garde painters of his era, he and his Tiffany School began to develop a newer botanical style that looked directly toward the Art Nouveau movement, which was soon to find its most brilliant practitioner in Tiffany & Co.'s founder's son, Louis Comfort Tiffany.

Art Nouveau was a highly manneristic art of purely decorative effects whose signature undulating whiplash curves were inspired by the gracefully and subtly reversing curves of Japanese water, vine, and floral patternings. These stylistic details accompany a palette of pale muted colors reminiscent of the simple colorways of textiles. The flora eventually favored by Art Nouveau was a loose collection of lilies and vines, not the least of which was the iris. Offering the requisite softly and sensually undulating patterns ready-made by Mother Nature, the tulip, the wisteria, the nasturtium, the magnolia, and, of course, the orchid would all be amply exploited by this "new art."

The Tiffany School's intense interest in orchids and magnolias, like its interest in Japanese woodblock prints fifteen years earlier, was in advance of its time in the late 1880s. In the two years preceding 1889, Paulding Farnham, by far the most able botanical artist working with Edward C. Moore, began to focus his orchid studies and, later, at the Paris Exposition, presented a series of twenty-four enameled gold orchid jewels in the Tiffany display, which won him a gold medal for his efforts at twenty-nine-years of age. Widely admired and publicized at the time, Farnham's orchids had a considerable impact on the course of later Art Nouveau

floral jewelry design and still rank amongst the greatest achievements in the history of jewelry.

The orchid theme for Tiffany's 1889 displays that included not only jewelry but also Edward C. Moore's enameled silver objects, most notably the Orchid Vase, a monument of silversmithing twenty-seven inches high and sixteen inches in diameter, with six splendidly enameled panels of interlacing early Art Nouveau orchids by Moore's other star student, John T. Curran. The silverwork also won a gold medal for Tiffany at the 1889 Exposition and contributed to Edward C. Moore being awarded the Legion of Honor in the same year.

The study of nature's flora in the Tiffany School was paying off in a big way for both Farnham and Curran, who had begun their apprenticeships at Moore's School around 1875, when both were teenagers. By 1889, both were established as two of America's finest decorative artists. Four years later, at the World's Columbian Exposition in Chicago (the United States's answer to the Paris Exposition of 1889), John T. Curran's extraordinary Magnolia Vase would win a gold medal and a place in American design history.

Edward C. Moore did not live to see the Magnolia Vase. John T. Curran's first botanical drawings for the flowers are signed and dated mid-to-late May 1891. Three months later, on August 2, Edward C. Moore died at the age of sixty-four, having barely begun work on Tiffany's designs for Chicago 1893. His two students, however, would not have disappointed him. Both Paulding Farnham's Tiffany jewels and John T. Curran's Tiffany silver took home gold medals.

Following the Chicago World's Fair, Paulding Farnham continued to delight the world of design with his floral jewels; most notably at the Paris Exposition of 1900, where a breathtaking nine-inch-long iris corsage ornament of blue Montana sapphires and green demantoid garnets played a leading part in again winning the gold medal for jewelry. The iris corsage ornament, now in the Walters Art Gallery in Baltimore, remains the greatest piece of nineteenth-century jewelry made in America. The year after the triumph of his jewelry designs in Paris, Farnham continued his floriform jewels with an equally large and glorious carnation ornament in pink tourmalines, diamonds, and demantoids for the Buffalo, New York, Pan-American Exposition of 1901, where he again won Tiffany the gold medal for jewelry.

The Paris and Buffalo fairs celebrated the dawn of a new century, which brought with it both an innovative vision of art and design and a new take on nature. Led by Edward C. Moore, Farnham and Curran were deeply rooted in the nineteenth century and in Japonisme, Symbolism, Post-Impressionism, and early Art Nouveau. During the 1890s, however, their work was overshadowed and ultimately eclipsed by the prodigious talents of the son of Tiffany & Co.'s founder, Louis Comfort Tiffany.

Tiffany & Co. had shared its exhibition space at the World's Columbian Exposition with Louis Comfort Tiffany's extraordinary stained-glass windows and glass mosaics, which won fifty-three prizes and brought the younger Tiffany the world recognition he deserved. By the time of the Paris Exposition of 1900, Louis Comfort Tiffany was also the world leader in Art Nouveau blown-glass design with his Favrile glass vases, and he had already introduced such enduring icons of design as his Dragonfly leaded-glass lampshade.

At the Paris and Buffalo expositions, the younger Tiffany was the anointed king of Art Nouveau glass, yet he still shared the spotlight with his father's head designer, Paulding Farnham. In 1902, however, Charles Lewis Tiffany died, leaving his son in control of the destiny of Tiffany & Co. The same year, Louis Comfort Tiffany appointed himself design director, dispossessing Farnham.

Turning away from the nineteenth-century infatuation with Orientalism, American design in the new century digressed from the exotic in nature toward a quite different attraction for nature's everyday species, found in the American countryside. The irises, magnolias, and

Leaves from Eugène Grasset's *La Plante et ses Applications Ornamentales*, a seventy-two-page folio published in 1897. Plates from this publication have been inspirations for Tiffany designers for over a hundred years.

Opposite: Louis Comfort Tiffany's leaded-glass Gourd-vine lampshade placed in front of his "Three Seasons" leaded-glass folding screen that he displayed at the 1900 Paris Exposition. The left panel's clematis vine represents spring; the center panel's gourd vine represents summer; the right panel's grapevine represents autumn. Gourds—symbols of fecundity—appear in Japanese paintings, prints, textiles, *tsuba* (sword guards), pottery, and glassware.

orchids gave way to American wildflowers and even to weeds and vines such as Queen Anne's lace, hawthorne, bittersweet, Virginia creeper, and dandelion. These commonplace flora were the subjects of Louis Comfort Tiffany's jewelry displayed by Tiffany & Co. at the St. Louis Louisiana Purchase Centennial Exposition of 1904.

Under Louis Comfort Tiffany's direction, the company's design department continued to draw and paint detailed studies of nature's more humble plants and flowers just as the apprentices and designers had studied more exotic flora under the new design director's original mentor, Edward C. Moore. Throughout his career in jewelry design, Tiffany continued to use his favorite interlacing vines, interpreted in gold and enamel, as surrounds for multicolored opals and other gemstones, recalling his celebrated Art Nouveau Favrile glass.

Louis Comfort Tiffany outlived his role in the world of design, which, following the end of World War I in 1918, moved on from the tendrils and undulating lines that Art Nouveau had borrowed from nature in favor of Art Deco's relentless geometric simplification of all it observed. After Louis Comfort Tiffany's death in 1933, a new design director was not appointed; rather, the design department came under the direction of Arthur LeRoy Barney, who briefly led Tiffany into the geometries of Art Deco and its offshoot, the 1940s Retro style.

In 1955, Tiffany & Co. was purchased by Walter Hoving (who also owned Tiffany's Fifth Avenue neighbor Bonwit-Teller), and the recently retired president of the Parsons School of Design, Van Day Truex, was chosen by Hoving as Tiffany's second design director. As Edward C.

Fleurage platinum and eighteen-karat gold bracelet and necklace, designed by Jean Schlumberger in 1958. Each flower is different; their centers are set with varicolored sapphires. The bracelet has 510 diamonds weighing a total of 15.01 carats; the necklace has 1,070 diamonds weighing 30.93 carats.

Moore and Louis Comfort Tiffany had been, Truex was a fanatical believer in nature as the source of all design and based many of his finest works on nature's humble leaves and seedpods. Unlike Louis Comfort Tiffany, however, he had no particular sympathy with floral patterns, preferring instead the Japanese woodblock printmakers who had inspired Edward C. Moore.

One year after becoming design director, in 1956, Truex brought the great French jewelry designer and fellow passionate admirer of nature, Jean Schlumberger, to Tiffany. Schlumberger's designs were very much a product of the glamorous world of fashion, society, and art of Paris of the 1930s. He had begun his career in jewelry design in 1937 making costume jewelry for the couturière Elsa Schiaparelli, a genius who surrounded herself with the period's more social Surrealist artists such as Salvador Dalí, Leonor Fini, Roberto Matta, and Serge Matta. In this milieu, Schlumberger developed a taste for the idiosyncratic and exotic sides of nature's flora and fauna, which would inform his designs throughout his career.

There is no record of Jean Schlumberger's knowledge of the work of Louis Comfort Tiffany, yet Louis Comfort Tiffany's jewelry department had remained open at Tiffany & Co. until mid-1933, only four years before Schlumberger began designing jewelry. Furthermore, in 1929, the twenty-two-year-old Schlumberger had been sent by his wealthy, textile-producing French family to work in the then-thriving New Jersey textile industry, in order to gain experience. It would be difficult to believe that, while involved in the world of New Jersey textiles, whose designers were very much in contact with the world of art and design of New York City just across the Hudson River, the artistically inclined young Schlumberger had not taken time to visit Tiffany & Co.'s great Italianate store on Fifth Avenue and Thirty-seventh Street. There he would have seen the display of Louis Comfort Tiffany's jewelry, whose mixtures of precious, semiprecious, and not-at-all-precious materials could be viewed as approaching proto-fashion jewelry design. Whatever the case, echoes of Louis Comfort Tiffany's highly sophisticated taste for nature can be found among Schlumberger's designs. Perhaps it comes as no coincidence that, in 1929, Mr. Tiffany's chief collaborator in art jewelry design for the previous fifteen years, Meta Overbeck, had been, like him, a member of the design department of a New Jersey silk manufactory before joining Tiffany.

Louis Comfort Tiffany drew on both Mother Nature's simpler as well as on her more exotic aspects in his designs, and Jean Schlumberger's fondness for the exotic and idiosyncratic was a perfect complement at Tiffany & Co. to Van Day Truex's love of nature's simpler side. Schlumberger's quintessentially sophisticated, sometimes surreal, and always fanciful interpretations of nature's exotica inspired Tiffany's next name jewelry designer, Donald Claflin, to draw his own extravagant versions of nature's flora and fauna, inspired more by myth than by reality.

Claflin's extraordinary jewels were soon balanced by the work of his talented young associate (and later name jewelry designer), Angela Cummings, whose sensibility was more in line with Van Day Truex's bent for simplicity. Turning away from Claflin's sumptuous and mythological view of nature, Cummings found her inspiration in humble leaves and flower petals.

In 1974, the most influential jewelry designer of our times, Elsa Peretti, arrived at Tiffany & Co. with a passion for both nature and the arts of Japan to rival Edward C. Moore's. Like Moore, Peretti was thoroughly knowledgeable about European, American, and Japanese art and design but, reflecting twentieth-century modernism's mistrust of ornament, Peretti pared down nature to significant form, refining and abstracting whatever in nature caught her selective eye and bringing out in her designs a compelling sensuality that is, of course, always present in nature, even if it passes unnoticed by a less incisive eye.

In nature's simplest creations, Elsa Peretti sees symbols of growth and regeneration and imbues them with requisite sensuality. Accomplishing this with her unparalleled vitality and stylishness, she reaffirms that, after all is said and done, "Mother Nature is the best designer."

Drawing for the cover of Tiffany's 1885 catalogue. The background of lilac florets suggests that it was drawn by the twenty-
five-year-old Paulding Farnham, whose c. 1887 Lilac brooch
appears on page 51.

Andō Hiroshige's 1857 color
woodblock print entitled *Iris
at Horikiri.* Irises in the work
of Hiroshige and Hokusai
inspired Edward C. Moore's
silver designs.

Irregularly shaped Japan-
esque silver flask with an
applied gold iris designed by
Edward C. Moore. Its drawing in Tiffany's archives is
dated August 23, 1881.

Above: Etching design, by Edward C. Moore, dated January 3, 1881, for a Japanesque silver cup decorated with irises.

Below: Enameling design for a silver card case, c. 1876. The peony pattern was probably inspired by textile patterns in Japanese books called *shōe.*

Opposite: Japanesque silver water pitcher decorated with irises designed by Edward C. Moore in 1878. Most of the decoration is etched; the insects and some of the flowers' stems and centers are applied gold. The body's surface is hand hammered, reducing its shine and emphasizing the etched and applied decoration. The hexagonal hammering is characteristic of Tiffany silver in the late 1870s and 1880s.

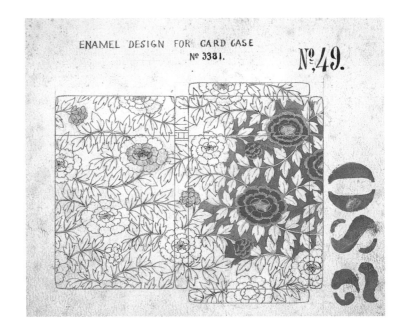

Unsigned drawings in the
Tiffany archives showing
the front and back of a
sunflower, c. 1890. These
exceptional drawings are
probably John T. Curran's
preparatory studies for an
unrealized work in enam-
eled silver for the World's
Columbian Exposition held
in Chicago in 1893.

Enamel-on-gold, diamond, and platinum brooch in the form of a mignonette *(Reseda odorata)*, designed by Paulding Farnham for the 1889 Paris Exposition. The Paris edition of *The New York Herald* commented, "It is simply marvelous, the stamens being only the thinness of a hair, yet having two colours in enamel, while even the smallest part of the flower is reproduced." The illustration at top and the archival photograph at bottom date from 1889.

Opposite: Enamel-on-gold vinaigrette (scent bottle) in the form of a trumpet-vine flower. The silver stopper, representing the berry, is set with diamonds. Designed by Paulding Farnham for the 1889 Paris Exposition.

STUDY of CULTIVATED

FORGET ME NOTS

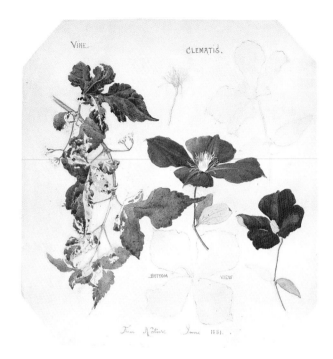

VINE.

CLEMATIS.

BOTTOM VIEW

From Nature June 1881

STUDIES OF MOUNTAIN ASH
SEP 27TH '82

Opposite, left: Study of cultivated forget-me-nots drawn by John T. Curran in 1892.

Opposite, right: Watercolor study labeled *August Lilies.* The aggressively bold composition suggests that it was the work of John T. Curran.

Above: Watercolor study of a clematis vine and blossoms labeled *From Nature* and dated June 1881.

Below: Watercolor study of a mountain ash dated September 27, 1881.

Overleaf, left to right: Study of a cockscomb *(Celosia cristata)* dated September 1, 1882, probably drawn by John T. Curran, who was twenty-three at the time. His taste in nature's flowers tended toward either large-scaled and robust varieties such as magnolias or humble garden plants like forget-me-nots.

Watercolor labeled *Moetrosideros study,* or *Iron wood,* dated August 1882.

Watercolor study of asters dated September 7, 1903.

Watercolor study of honeysuckle dated October 1, 1906.

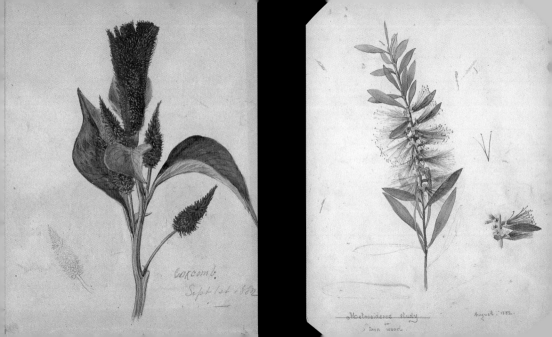

Cockscomb.
Sept 1st 1882

Metrosideros study
or
Iron wood.

August 1882.

veins beneath

7 — Sept — '08

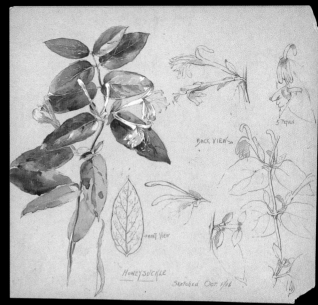

5 PETALS

BACK VIEW

FRONT VIEW

HONEYSUCKLE

Sketched Oct 1/06

43

Contemporary stylized floral
brooches loosely based on
Paulding Farnham's designs of
1885–1900.

Left to right across the spread:
Floral spray set with diamonds;
daisy with a dogtooth-pearl
flower and tsavorite-pavé leaves;
diamond flowers with tsavorite-
pavé leaves; spray of American
pink conch pearls and diamonds;
Queen Anne's lace in diamonds
with tsavorite leaves.

Study of a Shasta daisy, c. 1890 by Paulding Farnham,
Tiffany's primary jewelry designer from the mid-1880s
until 1901. Although Farnham is not known to have
designed daisy jewelry, Tiffany silver designer John T.
Curran designed an enamel-on-silver vase decorated
with daisies for the World's Columbian Exposition held
in Chicago in 1893.

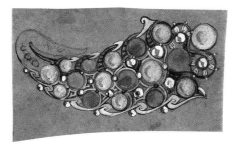

Above left: Archival photograph of Paulding Farnham's freshwater pearl, diamond, and enamel brooch shown at the 1889 Paris Exposition.

Below: Farnham's drawings for the brooch. *The Jewelers' Weekly* reported, "An enameled brooch of conventional design, set with ten large American pearls and five diamonds of moderate size, is very handsome. The brooch, particularly the enameled parts representing flowers and foliage, is plentifully studded with small brilliants and it is an elegant jewel."

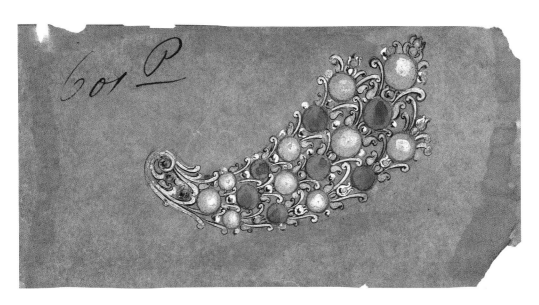

Opposite: Louis Comfort Tiffany's leaded-glass Wisteria lampshade, 26 inches in diameter, on a tree trunk bronze base. This popular lampshade was designed in 1901 by Mrs. Curtis P. Freshel, whose house in Chestnut Hill outside Boston was surrounded by wisteria vines.

Left: Photograph of wisteria blossoms by Charles Aubry. from Edward C. Moore's Tiffany School teaching collection 1864.

Opposite, above: Enamel-on-gold, diamond, and ruby Cactus brooches designed by Donald Claflin about 1968. Claflin's work was influenced by Jean Schlumberger; he designed jewelry for Tiffany from 1965 to 1975.

Opposite, below: Coral and diamond-pavé clips formed as an apple and a pear designed by Jean Schlumberger in 1964.

Above: Paulding Farnham's c. 1887 Lilac brooch of enamel florets with diamond centers placed upon his drawings for the brooch.

Below: Contemporary raspberry and lilac brooches. The raspberries are rubies and diamonds, the leaf is studded with tsavorites. The diamond-and-gold lilac brooch is based on Paulding Farnham's Lilac brooch above.

Paulding Farnham's c. 1890s
drawing for a gold mount on a
carved cameo-glass vinaigrette
made by Thomas Webb & Sons
in Stourbridge, England. Webb's
cameo-glass was imported by
Tiffany & Co. throughout the
1880s and 1890s.

Opposite: Eighteen-karat inlaid
gold Cyclamen bracelet, colored-
stone Rose Petal earrings, and
Ginkgo Leaf brooch, designed
by Angela Cummings c. 1980.
The Cyclamen bracelet was
inspired by cyclamen patterns
in Eugène Grasset's *La Plante et
ses Applications Ornamentales*,
published in 1897 (see page 24).
Cummings designed jewelry for
Tiffany & Co. from 1967 to 1983.

Above: Archival photograph of Louis Comfort Tiffany's Belladonna brooch made for the 1904 Louisiana-Purchase Exposition held in St. Louis.

Right: Jean Schlumberger's similar Cocoa Bean clip of eighteen-karat gold set with rubies and yellow beryls.

Below: A Louis Comfort Tiffany bar brooch with enamel-on-gold nasturtiums and an oval cabochon serpentine from New Jersey at the center. Probably made between 1905 and 1910.

Opposite: Drawing for an enamel-on-copper box decorated with nasturtiums, by Julia Munson, who worked on Louis Comfort Tiffany's enamels and jewelry from 1898 to 1914.

Millefiore Favrile glass vase,
3 5/8 inches tall, made by
Louis Comfort Tiffany's glass
factory, probably in 1902.
The term *millefiore* (thousand
flowers) refers to the ancient
Roman technique of repre-
senting flowers with disks
made from sections of glass
cane; the technique was
rediscovered by Venetian
glass makers in the sixteenth
century. This vase's classic
shape, subdued colors, and
silvery luster set it apart from
the eccentric shapes, strong
colors, and complex surfaces
of many other Louis Comfort
Tiffany vases. Its floral pattern is closely related to the
flowering vines in his leaded-glass windows, as well as
the gold and enamel vines
surrounding gemstones in
his Tiffany & Co. jewelry cre-
ated between 1904 and 1914.

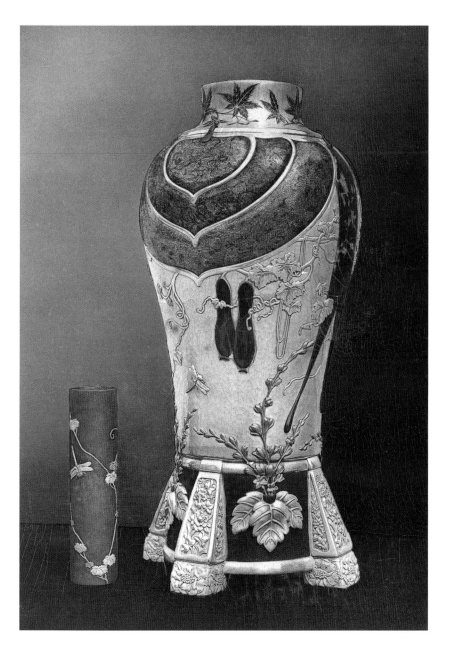

Hand-colored 1878 photo-
graph of a steel and silver
vase and the 20¼-inch-tall
Conglomerate Vase, the most
important work of Japan-
esque silver that Tiffany &
Co. showed at the 1878 Paris
Exposition. The vase has
applied decoration of niello,
copper, and gold, along with
the Japanese alloys *sentoku*
and *mokume*. Its decoration
includes Japanese maple
leaves and seedpods,
paulownia leaves and vines
(symbols of the Japanese
emperor), gourds, flowers,
flower-buds, a butterfly, and
a dragonfly. John T. Martin,
a collector of Barbizon
School paintings, purchased
the vase at the exposition
and displayed it prominently
in the picture gallery of his
house in Brooklyn.

Late-nineteenth century photographs from Florence in a Tiffany School botanical album.

Left: A hybrid cineraria cultivated by Giovanni Chiari in the Torrigiani garden.

Opposite: An orchid labeled *Aerides odaratum purpurem.*

567.

N? FIRENZE-GIARDINO TORRIGIANI   GIARDINIERE GIOVANNI CHIARI.

79   - C I N E R A R I A   H Y B R I D A -

435.

Nº   FIRENZE-

-AERIDES ODORATUM PURPUREUM-

Louis Comfort Tiffany
enamel-on-copper pitcher
decorated with repoussé
arrowroot plants applied
with silver and gold. Tiffany
also used arrowroot motifs in
his leaded-glass lampshades.

Sterling-silver Art Nouveau-
style tea set decorated with
arrowroot made in 1996, and
based on designs by Louis
Comfort Tiffany and Albert
A. Southwick, c. 1905.

Paulding Farnham's masterful
watercolor and pencil drawing of
cattleya orchids with maidenhair
ferns, c.1889. The first important cattleya orchid in the United
States was imported by prominent
New York florist Isaac Buchanan
in 1840. They were collected as
symbols of wealth and prestige
in the Gilded Age (1870–93).

The twenty-four jeweled and enameled orchid brooches that Paulding Farnham designed for Tiffany's display at the 1889 Paris Exposition achieved wide acclaim. Following up on this success, Tiffany displayed forty orchid brooches designed by Farnham at its New York store in 1890.

Opposite: Paulding Farnham's 1890 enamel-on-gold brooch representing a *Cattleya bicolor*, an orchid native to Brazil. The border of the labellum (lip) is diamond-pavé, and the diamond-pavé stem is studded with emeralds.

Above: Paulding Farnham's study of a *Phalaenopsis stuartiana* (native to Indonesia) for Orchid Brooch Number 68.

Below: Illustrations of orchid brooches from the *United States Commissioner's Report on the 1889 Paris Exposition*. The commissioners noted, "Tiffany & Co. obtained a gold medal, being in that respect placed on the same level as the best French jewelers, such as Fouquet, Rouvenat, Gross, Aucoc, Moche, etc. . . . All Americans will agree with us in congratulating Messrs. Tiffany & Co. on such brilliant and deserved success. It is an honor to them and to our country."

Right: Farnham's study for
the *Dendrobium nobile* brooch
opposite. This orchid is
native to the cool foothills
of the Himalayas.

Opposite: Orchid Brooch Number 44 depicts a *Cattleya schilleriana* native to Brazil's Esprito Santo mountains. The large, patterned column is studded with diamonds and the stem is diamond-pavé studded with emeralds.

Above: Contemporary orchid brooches inspired by Paulding Farnham's orchid brooches of 1889–90.

Left: Farnham's studies for two orchid brooches. The note was written by Edward C. Moore, who closely oversaw the design and production of all Tiffany silver and jewelry, including Farnham's orchid brooches.

42778

Brooch

Orchid like darker

Design but not quite as dark

Above left: Farnham labeled his drawing for Orchid Brooch Number 19 *Phalaenopsis Schillerianum* but it was probably an *Odontoglossum* native to the Philippines; this brooch was shown at the 1889 Paris Exposition.

Above right: Orchid Brooch Number 48. Farnham labeled his drawing *Odontoglossam crispum*. This brooch may represent an extinct variety or an early hybrid.

Opposite: Farnham's study for Orchid Brooch Number 67.

#67

Opposite: Double Daisy clip
of diamonds in platinum and
eighteen-karat gold, designed
by Jean Schlumberger in 1956.

Above: Fruit and Buds clip
designed by Jean Schlumberger
in 1962. The fruit is represented by sapphire-pavé; the
buds are tourmalines with
diamond-pavé calyxes. The
leaf is diamond-pavé.

"UMBRELLA" MAGNOLIA STUDY—
MAY 16. 91—

"UMBRELLA" MAGNOLIA
—MAY·18·91—

Opposite: John T. Curran's magnolia blossom study, c. 1891, for his monumental Magnolia Vase displayed at the World's Columbian Exposition in Chicago in 1893 (see page 79).

Above: Two more John T. Curran magnolia blossom studies for the Magnolia Vase, dated May 1891. The dates suggest that Edward C. Moore (who died August 24, 1891) may have overseen the beginnings of the Magnolia Vase.

John T. Curran designed the 31-inch-tall
Magnolia Vase for the 1893 Chicago Exposition. Tiffany's priced it at $10,000; its cata-
logue stated, "The decorations are chased in
relief work, and some treated in enameling.
Around the base of the vase are four large
pieces of opal matrix representing the earth,
out of which springs a latticework of cactus
leaves chased in high relief. These leaves are
divided into sections by perfectly wrought
goldenrod. The roots of the flower terminate
in scrolls encircling the opals. Above the
growth of cactus leaves and goldenrod, mat-
ted as a solid decoration around the widest
part of the vase, is a frieze of magnolias
enameled in natural size and colors, showing
all the delicate tints, with the soft, subdued
effect as in life." The vase was purchased by
the eighty-one-year-old Cornelia Ann
Atwill, who bequeathed it to the Metropolitan
Museum of Art in 1901.

Sterling-silver vases, candle holders, and covered jar made in 1992 by electroforming Louis Comfort Tiffany's ceramics. Tiffany himself made his Favrile bronzewares by electroforming his ceramic pieces between 1907 and 1914.

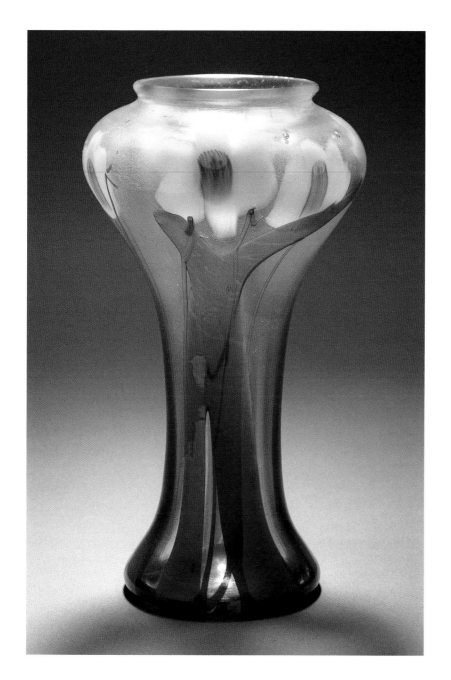

Opposite: The flowers in this
three-inch-tall paperweight
vase by Louis Comfort Tiffany
are jonquils and its interior
has an iridescent gold wash.
It was made in 1925.

Left: Louis Comfort Tiffany's
paperweight glass vase with
white narcissi; the interior has
an iridescent gold wash. It was
made in 1912.

Silver and inlaid-copper vase with wild roses and an abstract curvilinear pattern; designed c. 1910 by Albert A. Southwick, who worked as a silver designer at Tiffany from 1902 until he became manager of the company's Paris store in 1921.

Opposite: Silver and inlaid-copper loving cup displayed at the 1893 Chicago Exposition, eleven inches tall, undoubtedly designed by John T. Curran, the chief designer for the Tiffany silver display at the Chicago Exposition. The Tiffany catalogue listed it, "Love Cup, Greek Dolphin handles inlaid copper leaves." The sinuous vines show the influence of Edward Colonna, who worked briefly for Louis Comfort Tiffany in the 1880s and became a leading figure in the Art Nouveau movement.

Eighteen-karat gold Tulip
necklace with diamond-pavé
leaves and insects designed by
Jean Schlumberger in 1959 for
Mrs. William S. "Babe" Paley,
considered the most elegant
woman of her time.

Sumptuously extravagant
diamond-pavé and platinum
Leaves and Flowers necklace
designed in 1957 by Jean
Schlumberger for Campbell
Soup heiress Mrs. Nathaniel
P. (Elinor Dorrance) Hill.

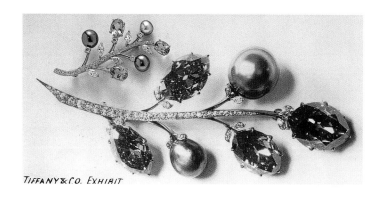

TIFFANY & CO. EXHIBIT

Above: South Sea cultured pearl, peridot, and diamond brooch based on the Paulding Farnham brooch in archival photo in the background.

Right: Floral brooches of diamonds and green, white, and golden South Sea cultured pearls. They were made in 2001 to commemorate the one-hundredth anniversary of Paulding Farnham's abstract floral jewelry made for the 1901 Pan-American Exposition in Buffalo, New York. Background: A Farnham design for the Buffalo Exposition.

Opposite: Contemporary ruby, sapphire, and diamond-pavé brooch resting on Paulding Farnham's designs for similar brooches for the 1901 Buffalo Exposition.

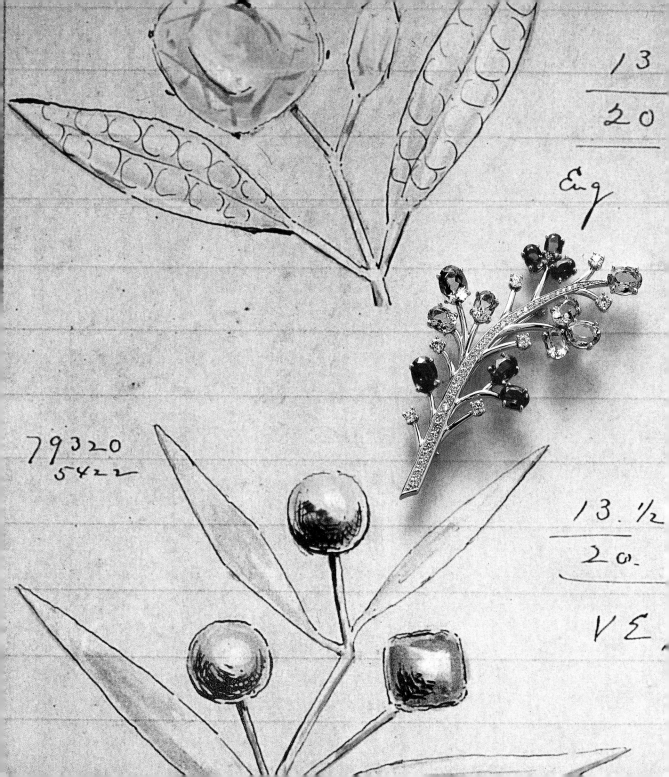

13
20

Eng

79320
5422

13. 1/2
20.

V E.

Tiffany's Garland pattern, introduced in 1990, is loosely based on Paulding Farnham's drawing for a maidenhair fern-motif necklace c. 1900.

Below: Portion of a Garland necklace and matching earrings of diamond and rubies set in eighteen-karat gold.

Opposite: Necklace of diamonds and sapphires set in platinum.

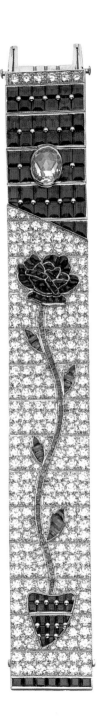

Above: Paulding Farnham's drawing for a rose lapel watch shown at the 1889 Paris Exposition.

Right: Platinum bracelet of diamonds and sapphires depicting a ruby-and-emerald rose growing from a ruby pot, c. 1930. Tiffany pieces in this exuberant Art Deco style are extremely rare.

Opposite: Enamel and diamond-pavé brooch depicting a rose beginning to bloom, designed by Paulding Farnham about 1890.

Foreground: Paulding Farnham presented this pink tourmaline and demantoid Iris brooch to his wife, Sally James Farnham. He based it on the Montana sapphire Iris brooch that he designed for the 1900 Paris Exhibition and is now at the Walters Art Gallery in Baltimore. *Background:* Irises from Charles Aubry's 1864 photograph album in the Tiffany archives.

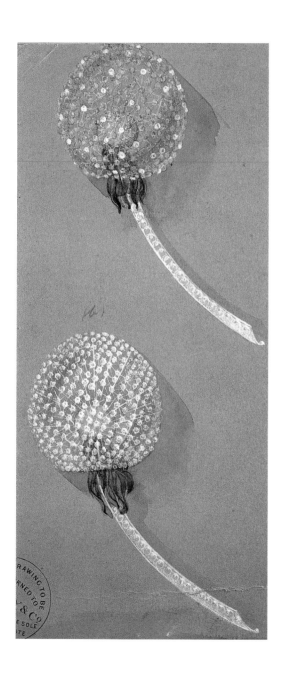

Paulding Farnham's designs for
jeweled dandelion seedballs (left)
and a Queen Anne's lace brooch
(above). Louis Comfort Tiffany
appears to have adapted these
designs for his dandelion seedball
and Queen Anne's lace hair ornament shown at the 1904 Louisiana
Purchase Exposition in St. Louis
(see following page).

TIFFANY & CO. EXHIBIT
LOUISIANA PURCHASE EXPOS
ST. LOUIS 1904

Left: Archival photograph of Louis Comfort Tiffany's Queen Anne's lace hair ornament and dandelion seed-ball shown by Tiffany and Co. at the 1904 St. Louis Exhibition. The hair ornament, now at the Metropolitan Museum of Art, has silver-and-copper stems, white enamel, and opal florets interspersed with demantoids, and three red garnets at the center. The seedball, now lost, was composed of fine silver wires terminating in small white opals.

Below: Louis Comfort Tiffany's c. 1914 octagonal enamel-on-silver inkwell decorated with Queen Anne's lace, one of his favorite motifs. George G. Booth, founder of the Cranbrook Academy of Art in Bloomfield Hills, Michigan, bought the inkwell for the Detroit Institute of Arts in 1920.

L. C. T. REG NO. 2823

March 21st 1940

may 1940

Floral jewelry designs dated 1940. The stylized, semi-abstract designs are characteristic of Tiffany & Co.'s venture into American Deco following the 1937 Paris Exposition.

9. NOV. 39

may 19/39

may 1940

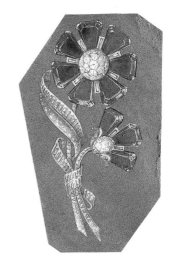

More floral jewelry designs
from the time of the 1939–
1940 New York World's Fair,
when Tiffany's opened its
present flagship store at
Fifth Avenue and 57th Street.
There were few purchasers
of lavish jewelry during the
Great Depression: the small
brooches with small gem-
stones at left reflect the eco-
nomic realities of the time.

Opposite: This design for a
heavy gold bracelet with sapphires and diamond pavé,
has a detachable flower that
could be worn as a brooch. It
was probably intended as an
exhibition piece at the 1939–
40 New York World's Fair.

4. DEC. 39

April 27th 1939

Japanesque coffee cup and saucer
designed by Edward C. Moore, c. 1881.
The cup's copper exterior has an
applied silver lotus pod, and the saucer
has a chased lotus pod and an applied
ladybug. Lotuses are traditional
Buddhist symbols for summer.

The Bryant Vase, designed by James H. Whitehouse and Eugene Soligny, was the most celebrated work of chased silver made in the United States. It was presented to the eighty-two-year-old nature poet and New York *Evening Post* editor William Cullen Bryant on June 20, 1876, and Tiffany & Co. displayed it at the Centennial Exhibition in Philadelphia shortly thereafter; Bryant gave it to the Metropolitan Museum of Art in 1877. In 1878, Tiffany made several electroformed copies of the vase and displayed one at the 1878 Paris Exposition. This photo of the pattern used for making the copies shows the corncob and wild rose decoration alluding to motifs in Bryant's poetry. Tiffany & Co. gave the pattern to the Metropolitan Museum.

This 8¾-inch-tall silver pitcher with Eugene J. Soligny's masterfully repoussé-chased spider chrysanthemums was made for the 1893 Chicago Exposition; it was probably designed by John T. Curran. The great Art Nouveau dealer Siegfried Bing wrote about Tiffany silver of the late 1880s and early 1890s, "Then new experiments took place with different processes. Repoussage produced knots of flowers in astonishingly high relief attenuated by chiseling whose fineness was pushed to the furthest possible extreme." The pioneering art, photography, and silver collector, Sam Wagstaff bought this pitcher for $2,640 at Christie's on January 23, 1982; his estate sold it for $35,200 at Christie's on January 20, 1989 to the Dallas Museum of Art.

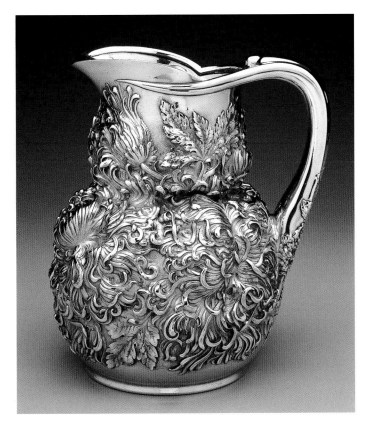

Paulding Farnham's studies
(at right and opposite) for
rosettes on a large diamond
corsage garniture and a carnation brooch of diamonds
set in oxidized silver for the
1889 Paris Exposition.

Below: Drawing for the cover of Tiffany & Co.'s 1883 catalogue issued in the autumn of 1882. The Japanese chrysanthemum (the traditional Buddhist symbol for autumn) suggests that it was drawn by the twenty-three-year-old Paulding Farnham, whose Japanese Chrysanthemum brooch was described in *New York Town Topics* on November 6, 1885: "A natural sized chrysanthemum made of purple and maroon-colored enameled gold is of the Japanese variety, having the thready, incurved petals. The disc of the flower is represented by a round, deep yellow diamond brilliantly cut." Tiffany & Co. displayed this chrysanthemum brooch at the 1889 Paris Exposition.

Opposite: Necklace of autumn leaves in fourteen-karat yellow gold, red gold, green gold, and copper, designed by Angela Cummings in 1980. The copper oak leaves were modeled on sample coppers struck silver dies made in Tiffany & Co.'s silver factory in the 1880s.

Above: 1890s study of a tulip-tree branch in flower; a tulip-tree leaf is at bottom right in the necklace opposite.

Leaf-and-flower sterling-
silver necklace, pendant,
earrings, and brooch
designed by Maurice Galli.

Opposite: Eighteen-karat hand-hammered maple-leaf necklace and earrings designed by Angela Cummings.

Above: Cummings's rose-petal necklace, earrings, and a pendant of hand-hammered yellow gold with red gold highlights.

Paulding Farnham's Chrysanthemum brooch of Unio dog-tooth pearls from the upper Mississippi River was made in 1904 for the flamboyant operetta star Lillian Russell (known as Diamond Lil).

Opposite: Contemporary floral brooch with enamel leaves, diamond-pavé petals, and South Sea pearl centers.

Floral brooch and earrings
of colored stone made in the
1950s. The gold stamens and
pistils are topped by diamonds.

Opposite: Pea Pod clip designed
by Jean Schlumberger in 1957.
The pea pods are jade, and the
eighteen-karat gold leaves are
set with diamonds, tsavorites,
and rubies. Strawberry clip
of rubies and diamonds also
designed by Schlumberger
in 1957.

Above: Donald Claflin's c.
1969 design for a raspberry
bracelet of rubies, diamonds,
green enamel, and gold.

Opposite: Vigne (grapevine)
necklace of amethyst grapes,
cabochon emerald and
diamond-pavé leaves, and
eighteen-karat gold vines.
Designed by Jean Schlum-
berger in 1960.

This page: Flower pins and
earrings with rock crystal
petals and gemstone centers,
designed by Paloma Picasso
in 1984.

Opposite: Floral jewelry
designed by Paloma Picasso
in 1984. The smoky quartz
pendant at left has diamond-
pavé calyx and an amethyst
drop; the rock crystal pendant at right has a diamond-
pavé calyx and a yellow beryl
drop. The smoky quartz
earrings have clips set with
diamonds and tsavorites;
the drops are citrines

Above: Carved rock crystal box,
with an eighteen-karat gold lid,
in the form of an apple, designed
by Elsa Peretti in 1977.

Opposite: Elsa Peretti's Apple
pendants in sterling silver, jasper
and jade, designed in 1978.

Opposite: Drawing for an enameled gold pendant watch in the form of an apple, c. 1890, possibly by Paulding Farnham, who designed a Strawberry pendant watch for the 1893 Chicago Exposition.

Below and opposite: Floral jewelry
designs in American Deco style,
designed at the time of the 1939–1940
New York World's Fair, when Tiffany
opened its present flagship store at
Fifth Avenue and 57th Street.

ACKNOWLEDGMENTS

The author and Tiffany & Co. would first like to thank William R. Chaney, chairman of Tiffany, and Michael Kowalski, president and chief executive officer of Tiffany's for their confidence and support. Mr. Kowalski's dedication to conservation perpetuates Tiffany & Co.'s traditional focus on nature as our primary source of inspiration in design and did much to encourage the concept of these volumes.

We would like to give special recognition to Eric Erickson for his vital contribution to every aesthetic aspect of *Tiffany Flora* and *Tiffany Fauna*; to Kay Olson Freeman whose insightful research clarified so much of the history of America's explorer-artists; and to Rollins Maxwell for his enlightening captions. These books would not have been realized without their so many remarkable contributions.

We are grateful to the director, manager of research services, and registrar of the Tiffany archives (Annamarie Sandecki, Louisa Bann, and Stephanie Carson) for contributing so much imagery and information to these works; to MaryAnn Aurora for keeping order throughout; to Eric Himmel, editor-in-chief of Harry N. Abrams for his support of all involved with the books' realization: Harriet Whelchel, our editor, and her assistant, Josh Faught, for their keen eyes and enthusiasm; Ellen Nygaard Ford, our designer at Abrams, for orchestrating diverse and complex imagery with imagination, vitality, and charm.

The books could not have been realized without the generous help of the New York Historical Society; The Metropolitan Museum of Art; The Museum of the City of New York; The Louis C. Tiffany Garden Museum, Matsue, Japan; The Morse Museum of American Art; The Detroit Institute of the Arts; The Dallas Museum of Art; The Doris Duke Charitable Foundation; Lillian Nassau, Ltd.; Christie's; Sotheby's; Phillips, de Pury & Luxembourg; Nelson & Nelson; A La Vieille Russie; Primavera Gallery; Historical Design; the Sataloff family; the Ellman family; Anka K. Palitz; Carolyn Staley; Mr. & Mrs. Richard Oughton; Carlo Eleuteri; and last but far from least the photographers: Hiro; David Kelley; Phil Garfield; and Walter Thomson.

EDITOR: Harriet Whelchel
EDITORIAL ASSISTANT: Josh Faught
DESIGNER: Ellen Nygaard Ford
PRODUCTION MANAGER: Shun Yamamoto

Library of Congress Cataloging-in-Publication Data

Loring, John.
  Tiffany / by John Loring.
    p. cm.
  ISBN 0–8109–4573–8 (set)
  1. Tiffany and Company. 2. Jewelry—United States—History—20th century. 3. Decoration and ornament—Plant forms. 4. Decoration and ornament—Animal forms. I. Title: Title of vol. 1: Tiffany flora. II. Title: Title of vol. 2: Tiffany fauna. III. Title.

NK7398.T5 A4 2003
739.27'09747'1—dc21
                    2002015524

Published in 2003 by Harry N. Abrams,
Incorporated, New York.
All rights reserved. No part of the contents
of this book may be reproduced without
written permission of the publisher.

Printed and bound in Japan

10 9 8 7 6 5 4 3 2

Harry N. Abrams, Inc.
100 Fifth Avenue
New York, N.Y. 10011
www.abramsbooks.com

Abrams is a subsidiary of
LA MARTINIÈRE
GROUPE

Endsheets: Unsigned drawings in the Tiffany archives showing the front and back of a sunflower, c. 1890.

Page 1: Floral clip designed by Jean Schlumberger in 1958. The diamond-pavé flower petals are centered by a large yellow sapphire; the ruby-pavé buds are sprinkled with tiny diamonds.

Pages 2–3: Floral brooch and earrings of colored stone made in the 1950s.

Pages 6–7: John T. Curran magnolia blossom studies for the Magnolia Vase (May 1891). The dates on these drawings suggest that Edward C. Moore (who died August 24, 1891) may have overseen the beginnings of the Magnolia Vase.